Uncertainly Sure

Lizette McMillen

Presentation by *BookLeaf Publishing*

Web: www.bookleafpub.com

E-mail: info@bookleafpub.com

ISBN: 9789357214643

First edition 2022

This is for the sad girl inside me who hadn't said a word in way too long because her thoughts were too loud to process. Let's not let that happen again.

ACKNOWLEDGEMENT

I've never been one to publicly name names but a handful of folks played key rolls in crafting these ramblings of my mind. Cheers to each of them* and thanks for the inspiration.

*This exludes anyone working at The Trust, because fuck those guys. They can all kick rocks.

PREFACE

I have always loved telling stories. Mostly true stories. My stories. At various points in my life, I considered myself to be a writer, but sometimes I'd also stop writing for years at a time. This was often due to hardship, to stress, and I would hold things away until they could no longer be contained and I would turn my strife into something beautiful. Rilke said the life of a poet is a lonely one, and I believe it. I don't much like being lonely, and I've fought like hell to make more of this all. But I do spend a lot of time inside my head and this has only increased over the last 4 years. I've been told that the only way out is through. So here I am, digging through thoughts and feeling and ideas, in writing, for the first time in over 4 years, trying to make something beautiful. Giving myself a voice again. I've missed this, telling my story in such an intimate way. And this time I'm sharing it with anyone in the world who will give it the time of day. It is both exciting and yet also a mortifying thing to do. If you are reading this, thank you, and try to be kind. xo

Today, Of All The Days

I could only imagine you in Portland, Seattle, or
Austin.
That's what he told me
On day one
After all the other days had passed.
I'm a very different person now than I was
All those years ago
(However many they have been).
But I'm still ME
And it feels good to be seen.
From late nights and long talks
Dissecting songs
Streaming shows
Musing over some manga
To questioning the odds
Like, does lightning strike twice?
Not often.
How often?
Just sometimes.
Like now.
Sometimes moving forward means looking
back.
If I'm going to jump
I'm going to need a net
And it looks like the world has my back lately.
Here's my first real step.

Passive Aggressive Magic Tricks

In another life,
I did this all the time.
It was like breathing,
Until it wasn't...
And then it was.
And then....
But here I am now,
Trying again
To catch my breath,
To find my voice,
Telling stories to the masses
In symbols and secrets,
Chasing all the lives I've ever dreamed to live,
Just trying to see what sticks,
What lines burn out,
Which paths rise
And which paths fall,
Acting with intention
Because there's no such thing as luck -
But a little happenstance never did hurt,
And I could use some more...
Because, yesterday, I was stuck,
Stranded in dichotomy,
A pit

Between fact-based confidence
And intrusive self-doubt.
I know better.
I'm told better.
It's the fear to try,
The fear to fly,
The fear
Of inevitable
CRASH!

Loss of Consortium

Deprivation of benefits
Of a family relationship.
That's what we have here.
But that claim still says pending.
A multi-page letter
Desperately pleading for grace
Apparently isn't what it takes
To convince paper pushers
Checking boxes for crooks
That we all were left broken that day.

I bridge these gaps
With phone calls and snaps
And tik toks of food we could make.
And, of course, those 12 hour drives
Sleeping roadside in the cold
To make it home by lunch.
Not that we have a home these days.
It's only home when we're together.
A handful of weeks each year,
When we used to have them all.

Take the kids to school.
An assiago bagel.
Buttered.

Hot chais.
What are your alternative milks?
Do you need any help?
I'm running errands.
Is there time for lunch today?
I've got work
But plan on dinner,
And dessert.
It's time for that show you like.
We're late!
Tomorrow!
Ok.

We haven't done that in 4 years
And we never will again.
But we're alright aren't we?
At least, that's what they'd like us to believe
While they line their pockets
With money earmarked for us.
And it's not about the money.
I hate the money,
That it comes down to this,
Because we lost more
Than they can dream
Of giving back...

But being able to pay the bills
Really wouldn't hurt my feelings.

Counting Down

I've stifled myself again
Overly ambitious
I can't bite that big
Dreams of grandeur
Bred in limitations
Choke the flame
Extinguish the fire
While anxiety watches
Time run out
I'm behind again
An unlikely finishline
Where will I be tomorrow?

Seafoam

Battery: 0
So why am I awake?
Funny how that works
Narcolepsy and insomnia
Comorbidities that can't agree
A bed of foam
I feel like I'm floating
How long can I resist
Or do I even have that option?
6 out of [more than] 36
I can feel my face again
Being tired is my most common high
But so much less funny
All I can think is how
The mechanist
Didn't sleep
For a year

More Than I Can Handle

I could quote Mom Jeans. any day
An accurate representation
Because I'm always in over my head
A tendency that tends to trend
With us neurodivergent types
It makes us anxious and awkward
I wouldn't say that's always bad
But damn
It sure is tiring

Eleventh Hour

9

11 in 10
I'm a third of the way
And an hour remains
I tell myself, "I told you so"
And also, "there's still time!"
Why is every day like this?
I still haven't stopped the mail

Mouth Feel

If you knew
How often I rewrite
A script I'll never say...
My memory
It fails me
I rework it out
My talking points get lost
I'll add others
Maybe the words
Just aren't right
BUT
I can be so quick
And concise
When I'm sharing
With the world
Here's my heart
In a blender
My mind
All mixed up
For you
When I should be
Crafting a slow pour
Something for you
To savor
I guess I just enjoy

The texture
Of unfiltered vulnerability

I'd Cross The World To Keep You (But I Know I Can't)

I'm playing Paper Thin Walls
On loop in my mind
As I listen
To muffled dialogue
And wonder
How long I'll get to do this
And all the other
Minor annoyances
We let ourselves resent
Until they're gone.
The very idea
Of your absence
Is terrifying.
It's also guaranteed.
So I'll lay here
And listen to you talk
When I'd like to be asleep
Because one day
I know
These walls
Will be silent
At night.

Off Limits

There are some wounds
I wasn't aware of
Topics that are too raw
Too sensitive to touch
And I'm sure there are more
Yet to come
I don't want to cry
Because I already did
For that other one
That I wasn't planning to face
Tonight
So this one will have to stay
Tucked away
Filed with stars
Because it really IS important
But I don't have the bandwidth
Tonight
And I've learned
The importance
Of healthy boundaries
Even with just myself
If I intend
To sustain
My sanity

Balance

Pull me
Out of my mind
Reel me
Back to
Some semblance
Of sense
Hold me
Accountable
And also
In your arms
Because
I don't think
That I get
Enough hugs

A List Of People That I Need To Call

I've had
A broken tooth
For nearly
Two years
And
I'm not
The only
One

I kept
The message
From
The clinic
(From both)
So
I won't
Lose
The number

Is my
Insurance
Up to date?
I'm almost
Positive
It's valid

Or they
Would not
Have called.

If I establish
I'll need to
Contact California
For records
I've never
Been
Informed on
(I wonder
What that
Last test
Told them)

I'm going
To need
Referrals:
Psychiatric
A sleep study
I probably
Need glasses
By now

This
List
Is
Incomplete

I've Forgotten How To Count

I've got a whole alphabet
Of diagnostics
To dazzle you
While trying to explain myself
A list of letters
To tell you why:
I am forgetful
I appear to be lazy
I didn't eat
OR
I ate too much
OR
I only ate junk
Why:
I couldn't sleep
OR
I overslept
How:
I lost track
AND
I'm late again
Why:
I bought the thing
That I didn't need
And why:

I can't get off my screen
And many more
The list goes on
Let's just say it's endless
I'm an all around hot mess
I just need to know:
If you care enough
To try
To understand
OR
If I'm just
Wasting
My breath

That's One Big Dandelion

Home is not a location.
That is only a house.
Or maybe an apartment...
Perhaps a trailer?
Don't be so pedantic.
You know what I mean.
Home is made
Of thoughts
And feelings
And memories
And people
We think fondly of.
Home is made
Of love
And comfort,
A place
To feel safe.
While, indeed,
It is nice
When some location
Can corroborate
And accommodate
Both
That is not always the case.
I only realized recently

How much
I long
For a house
That could house
My home
Instead of being scattered
Like wishes
In the wind.

Second Thought

The creative process
For intimate arts
Presents a conundrum
With no easy answer
When other people
Become your content

It's true
That this is my story to tell
But how can I
When it includes you
And you haven't behaved well?

On the one hand
I am only being honest
And to do so is entirely fair
But on the other
I don't think you'd think it was nice
I would hate to make things awkward

Disagreements don't mean
I don't value what we have
Good friends are hard to find
And I don't really want to replace you
(What an ordeal,

And maybe even impossible)

I think I'll keep
That one
To myself

This Is Easier To Fix Than My Chemical Imbalance But It's Still Gonna Cost Me Money

I woke up
Feeling
The aesthetic
Imbalance
Of the ink
In my skin

5 right
1 mid
1 left

And
While I've always
Planned
To have more
The want
Or need
To do so
Is now
URGENT

Must
Get
More

Maybe I'm Just Delusional

I've often wondered
If
The faces cars make
While careening
'Cross the countryside
Is on purpose
Or if
My pareidolia
Is simply
Top teir
But I know
Last night
I was tired
Because
That's always
When it's worst
(Best?)
Yes
The cars
Of course
And some houses
Wide eyed
Counting commuters
But I swear
Every rig

On the 5
Last night
Had a face
On its 2
Back
Doors

Sometimes Our Brains Know What We Need

You know
You're stressed
When responsibilities
Sneak
Into
Your dreams

Last night
(This morning)
I dreamt
About this book
About the deadline
About having passed it

But I also dreamt
That I
Wasn't
The only one

Chances are
That Marco
Is NOT
Also
Writing a book

BUT

It made me
Feel better
Anyway

I guess I'll
Proceed
Now

I Don't Need Capitalism To Work Myself Into The Ground

There's an urge
To maximize
Every project
When I could
Easily
Just
Be done
And sometimes
I settle
Because I'm
Out of time
Or out of cash
Or out of fucks to give
But
If I can help it
If there's a way
To do more
To be more
To push myself
That extra inch
Then maybe
I can go

Another mile
Maybe I can make
Another day
Maybe I can create
More beauty
More life
And this
Burnout
Will be worth it

Risk Assessment

It's strange
Finding myself
My voice
In writing

The visuals
Say so much
That no one
Ever
Sees

That's what
Makes them
Safe

Those drawings
Tell a story
Of hope
Of resilience
Of a fight
For greater good
Of a better world
Imagined

I'm finding

My words
Feel
Like the opposite

The sad poet
A confused philosopher
Who knows
But doesn't
And isn't certain
What to do

Maybe it's the
ADHD anxiety
My PTSD
In action
Just a string
Of dysthymic thinking

At least I know it's not regret

One Off

The title of this poem
Is a lie
But poem 3
Isn't for you
Or me, really
It was always
On a different path
Headed to Seattle
An unexpected gesture
With purpose
And drive
A big fish
If you will
And poem 14
Became poem 13
And well
That's just bad luck

www.ingramcontent.com/pod-product-compliance
Lightning Source LLC
LaVergne TN
LVHW010931200726
843509LV00013B/2177